Workbook

New International Edition

Grade 1

T0385808

Tara Lievesley, Deborah Herridge
Series editor: John Stringer

WAYS LEARNING

PEARSON

Pearson Education Limited is a company incorporated in England and Wales having its registered office at Edinburgh Gate, Harlow, Essex, CM20 2JE.

Registered company number: 872828

www.pearsonglobalschools.com

Text © Pearson Education Limited 2012

First published 2003. This edition published 2012.

20 19
IMP 15 14 13 12 11 10

British Library Cataloguing in Publication Data

A catalogue record for this book is available from the British Library

ISBN 978 0 435133 69 6

Edited by Anna Woodford and Janice Curry
Designed by Ian Foulis
Original illustrations © Pearson Education Limited, 2003, 2009, 2012
Illustrated by Ian Foulis, Steve Evans and and Shelagh McNicholas
Cover photo/illustration © Alamy Images
Printed in Malaysia (CTP-VVP)

Acknowledgements

The authors and publisher would like to thank the following individuals and organisations for permission to reproduce photographs:

(Key: b-bottom; c-centre; l-left; r-right; t-top)
Fotolia.com: 24 (bucket), 24 (bucket & spades), 24 (cutlery), 24 (jar), 24 (kettle), 24 (Lego bricks), 24 (Orange bag), 24 (Scarf), 24 (stacking toy); **Pearson Education Ltd:** Trevor Clifford 7; **Shutterstock.com:** 5cl, 24 (Gold Bar), 24 (Wooden Spoon)

All other images © Pearson Education

Every effort has been made to contact copyright holders of material reproduced in this book. Any omissions will be rectified in subsequent printings if notice is given to the publishers.

Contents

What's alive?

1 Circle the living things.

2 Count the living things on this page. How many are there?

WS 2

Living and eating

1 What does a cat eat? Draw it here. Where does it live?

_____

_____

2 What does a sheep eat? Draw it here. Where does it live?

_____

_____

3 What does a bird eat? Draw it here. Where does it live?

_____

_____

4 What does a child eat for breakfast? Draw it here.

Where does a child live? _____

5 What are healthy foods to eat and drink for breakfast? _____

_____

_____

Name: _____ Date: _____

My senses

Draw the eyes, ears, mouth and nose on the face.

Draw the other hand.

Write or draw in the boxes.

I see with my

I hear with my

I taste with my

I smell with my

I touch with my whole body!

Growing older

1 Number these pictures in the right order. Write a number in each box.

2 Guess their age! Write your guess next to each person.

1 Less than ____ year old	More than ____ years old
About ____ years old	About ____ years old
About ____ years old	About ____ years old

3 How are they alike? How are they different? Talk to your friend.

WS 5

Who feeds where?

Complete the sentences

1

I feed from _____.

I _____ from place to place.

2

I eat _____.

I _____ from place to place.

3

I feed on _____ and _____.

I _____ from place to place.

4 Now draw your own small animal, and complete the sentences.

I eat _____.

I _____ from place to place.

Unit 1 Assessment

1 My five senses are _____

_____ .

2 Safia has a pet rabbit.

What must the rabbit have to live? Tick (✓) them.

3 Join the baby animal to its parent with a line.

4 Circle the things that are alive.

What plants need to grow

1 Underline two things this plant needed to grow well.

light   soil   noise
water   food

2 Underline two things this plant needs to grow better.

water   food   soil
light   sleep

3 Label the parts of this plant.

_____   _____

_____   _____

WS 8

How does a plant grow?

1 Put these pictures in the right order. Write a number in each box.

2 Write the correct label next to each picture:

stem   fruit   root   shoot   leaf   seed

[ ] _____

[ ] _____

[ ] _____

[ ] _____

[1] _____

[ ] _____

Growing game

Roll a dice. Read the box. Move your counter.

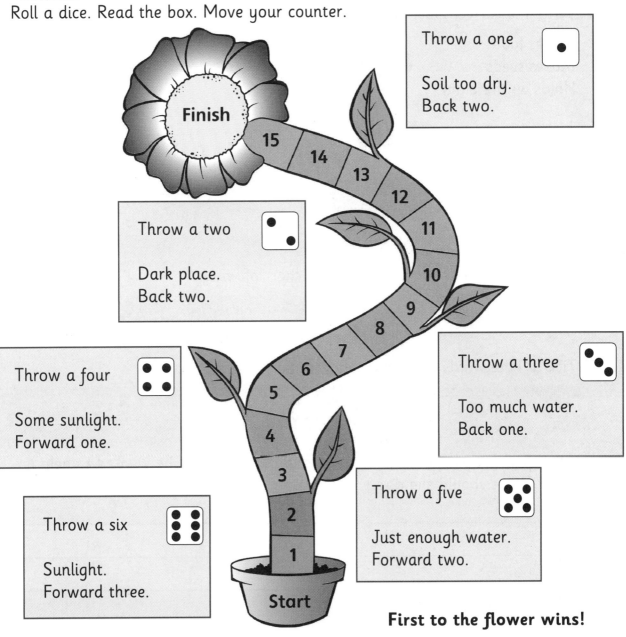

Throw a one

Soil too dry.
Back two.

Throw a two

Dark place.
Back two.

Throw a three

Too much water.
Back one.

Throw a four

Some sunlight.
Forward one.

Throw a five

Just enough water.
Forward two.

Throw a six

Sunlight.
Forward three.

First to the flower wins!

Name: _____ Date: _____

Unit 2 Assessment

1 Write the correct label on each line:

Makes food
Makes seeds
Holds up the plant

_____

_____

_____

2 Tick (✓) the words for a plant that is short of water.

healthy   yellow   limp   straggly   wilted   green

3 Tick (✓) the words for a plant that is short of light.

healthy   yellow   limp   straggly   wilted   green

4 Anna found a pot plant. It was in a dark, dry corner. She wanted to help it grow. What should she do?

_____

_____

_____

What's the material?

Draw a line from the picture to the name.

Then draw a line from the name to the material. The first one has been done for you.

Pictures	Names	Materials
	sheep	
	puddle	wood
	tree	plastic
	bucket	metal
	wave	wool
	door	water
	car	

Materials board game 1

A game for 2–3 players.

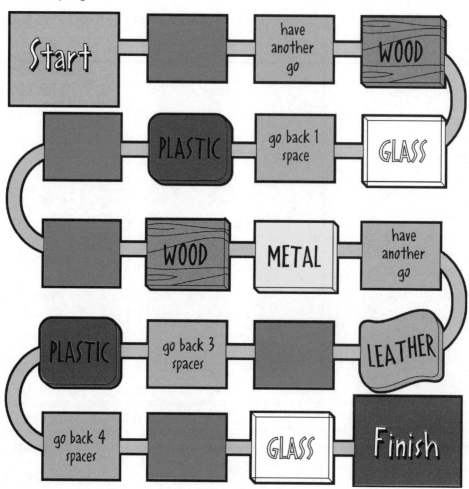

How to play

Throw the dice to move from **start** to **finish**.

If you land on a material square, name one thing made of that material. If you can't, you miss a go.

You cannot repeat what someone else has already said.

Materials board game 2

A game for 2–3 players.

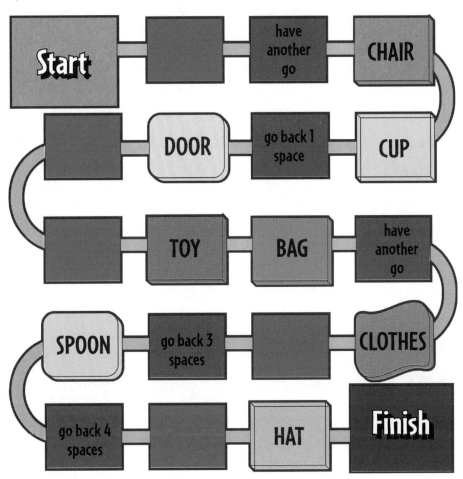

How to play

Throw the dice to move from **start** to **finish**.

If you land on an object square, name one material it is made from. If you can't you miss a go.

Your material for an object must be different from your friend's.

WS 14

Unit 3 Assessment

1 Circle the words that name a material.

> wood   cup   plastic   metal   spoon

2 Complete these sentences.

Wood is usually _____.

Metal feels quite _____.

Wool or fur feels _____.

Glass is used for making _____.

Paper is made from _____.

3 Draw a line to match the material with the object.

wood   door

metal   jumper

wood   tin can

4 Write the names of four or five materials to go in these groups.

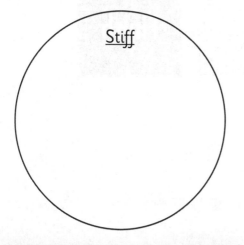

Stiff

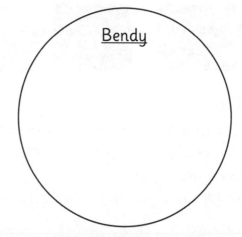

Bendy

WS 15

Pushes and pulls

Circle the pushes.

Draw a square round the pulls.

WS 16

Forces change things

1 Abed wants to go faster!
What should he do?
Tick (✓) the box.

Pedal softer ☐

Turn the handlebars ☐

Pedal harder ☐

2 Saleema wants to go round the corner.
What should she do?
Tick (✓) the box.

Pedal softer ☐

Turn the handlebars ☐

Pedal harder ☐

3 Mr Shah is driving.

To slow down, he would

_____

To go round the corner he should

_____

4 How do trains go round corners?

_____

_____

WS 17

Making a weathervane

1 Trace the arrow onto card.

2 Cut it out.

3 Tape it onto a cotton spool.

4 Cover one end of the spool with Plasticine.

5 Put the reel on a thin stick, like a pencil.

6 Hold the weathervane in the wind.

What did you find? Which way did the arrow point?

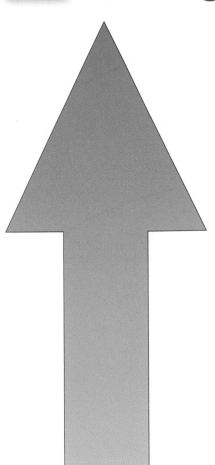

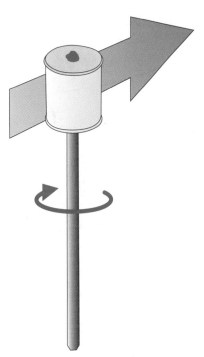

Unit 4 Assessment

1 Write or draw three things in the sets below.

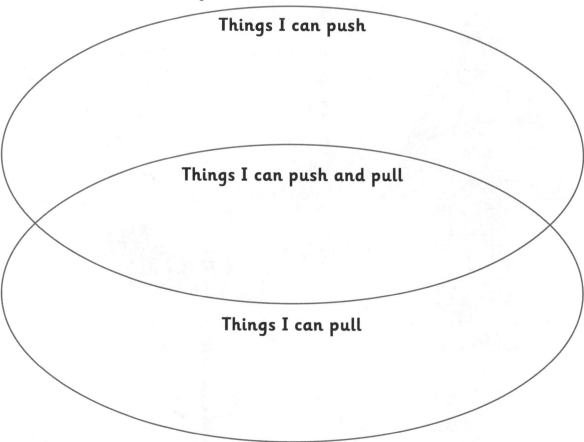

Things I can push

Things I can push and pull

Things I can pull

2 Draw a circle around the right answer in each sentence.

a) When I push the car harder, it goes

    further   **less far**

b) When I push the car gently, it goes

    further   **less far**

Say the sound

What do you do to each instrument? Write the word in the first column.

strike   tap   clash   pluck   blow

What sound does it make? Write the word in the second column.

strike   tap   clash   pluck   blow

The first one has been done for you.

When you	You hear
tap	ting

WS 20

Sounds like?

Teacher called the students.

Hassan was close to the teacher.

Anil was far away.

Dev was between them.

1 Who could hear the loudest?

_____

2 Who could hear nothing?

_____

3 Why was this?

_____

_____

Dal was behind the teacher.

4 Could Dal hear the teacher? _____

5 Hassan wrote about it. Fill in the spaces.

The further away, the _____ the sound.

The closer you are, the _____ the sound.

Sounds get _____ with distance.

Unit 5 Assessment

1 What sounds like this?

twang _____   bang _____

ping _____   tick _____

2 This is a xylophone. Write 'high' at the end of the xylophone that gives high notes. Write 'low' at the end that gives low notes.

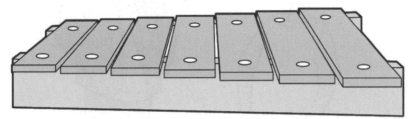

_____   _____

3 Join the start and end of each sentence.

We hear sounds   in all directions.

Quick vibrations   with our ears.

Something has to move   make high notes.

Sound spreads out   to make a sound.

4 You cover your ears with your hands. What happens to sounds?

_____

_____

Why? _____

_____

WS 22

How are they alike?

These two boys are in the same class.

1 Circle all the ways they are different.

2 How are they alike?

They have the same _____.

Their _____ looks the same.

They are both wearing _____.

How do they grow?

	Day 1	Day 2	Day 3	Day 4	Day 5
Plants under cloth					
Plants in sunlight					

One plant grew in the dark.

One plant grew by the window.

1 How are the plants alike?

Both have _____.

Both have _____.

2 How are the plants different?

The plant grown in the dark is _____ and

_____.

The plant grown in the light is _____ and

_____.

3 Why is the plant grown in the light different?

Because _____

_____.

Name the material

jar
_____
glass
_____

_____
_____

_____
_____

1 Name each object.

2 Name the material it is made from.

WS 25 Senses

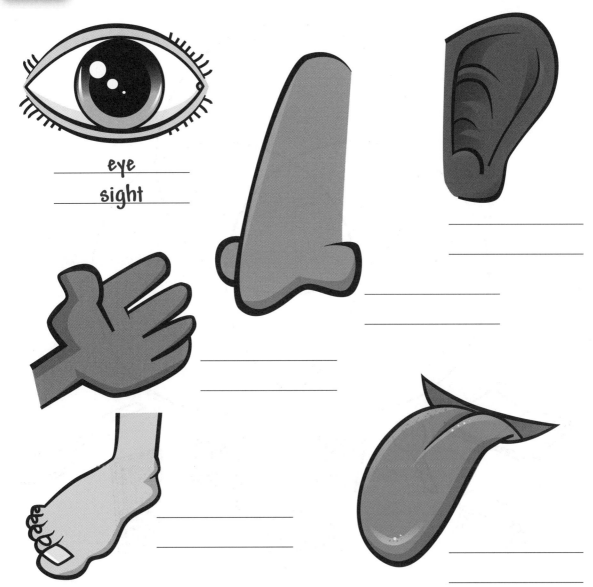

eye
sight

1 Name each body part.

2 Name the sense.

WS 26 Grouping materials

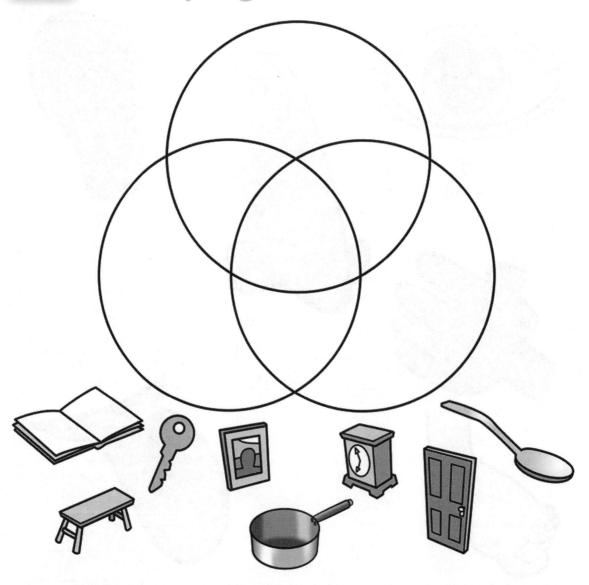

1 Draw the objects into the hoops. Put objects that are the same together. Some things belong in two hoops!

Naming materials

1 Draw the objects into the hoops again. Put objects that are the same together. Some things belong in two hoops!

2 Give a material name to each hoop. Use: metal   wood   paper

3 Give a material name to each overlap. Use:

metal and wood   paper and wood   metal and paper

4 Which overlap has nothing in it? _____